The Ultimate Guide To Organic Gardening

Organic Gardening For Beginners

James Gipson

This book is dedicated to anyone who is interested in organic gardening and considering creating their own organic garden.

Copyright Act of 1976, the scanning, uploading and electronic sharing of any part of this book without the explicit written consent or permission of the publisher constitutes unlawful piracy and the theft of intellectual property.

If you would like to use material or content from this book (other than for review purposes), prior written permission must be obtained from the publisher.

You can contact the publishing company at admin@speedypublishing.com. Thank you for not infringing on the author's rights.

Speedy Publishing LLC (c) 2014
40 E. Main St., #1156
Newark, DE 19711
www.speedypublishing.co

Ordering Information:
Quantity sales; Special discounts are available on quantity purchases by corporations, associations, and others. For details, contact the "Special Sales Department" at the address above.

This is a reprint book.

Manufactured in the United States of America

Table of Contents

Publisher's Notes i

Chapter 1: Introduction To Organic Gardening 1

Chapter 2: The Benefits Of Gardening Organically 3

Chapter 3: What Are The Risks Of Chemicals? 6

Chapter 4: The Theory Behind Organic Gardening 11

Chapter 5: How To Plan Your Garden 13

Chapter 6: Soil Preparation 16

Chapter 7: Planting Your Organic Garden 19

Chapter 8: Start Your Seeds Inside 22

Chapter 9: Organic Container Gardening 25

Chapter 10: Organic Hydroponic Gardening 28

Chapter 11: Weed Control 31

Chapter 12: Pest Control 36

Chapter 13: Common Garden Pests 40

Chapter 14: How To Make Your Own Compost 44

Chapter 15: Tending Your Garden 48

Chapter 16: Preparing Your Garden For Winter 54

Chapter 17: Bring Your Organic Plants Indoors For Year Round Growth 55

CHAPTER 18: NATURAL RECIPES FOR YOUR ORGANIC GARDEN 58

CHAPTER 19: CONCLUSION 62

MEET THE AUTHOR 64

MORE BOOKS BY JAMES GIPSON 66

Publisher's Notes

Disclaimer

This publication is intended to provide helpful and informative material. It is not intended to diagnose, treat, cure, or prevent any health problem or condition, nor is intended to replace the advice of a physician. No action should be taken solely on the contents of this book. Always consult your physician or qualified health-care professional on any matters regarding your health and before adopting any suggestions in this book or drawing inferences from it.

The author and publisher specifically disclaim all responsibility for any liability, loss or risk, personal or otherwise, which is incurred as a consequence, directly or indirectly, from the use or application of any contents of this book.

Any and all product names referenced within this book are the trademarks of their respective owners. None of these owners have sponsored, authorized, endorsed, or approved this book.

Always read all information provided by the manufacturers' product labels before using their products. The author and publisher are not responsible for claims made by manufacturers.

CHAPTER 1: INTRODUCTION TO ORGANIC GARDENING

For some people, gardening is a passion. Some people garden just as a hobby. For still others, it's a way to feed their families. We think Shirley MacClaine's character in "Steel Magnolias" said it best. "Because that's what Southern women do – we wear funny hats and grow things in the dirt."

You don't have to be from the South or be a woman, or even wear a funny hat to enjoy gardening. The thrill of seeing your first red, ripe tomato or watching your first stalk of corn reach from the ground can be an amazing experience for many people.

Gardening is also a great way to provide healthy food for you and your loved ones. When you buy produce from the store, it just isn't the same as presenting a salad to your family that came exclusively from your garden worked by your own two hands.

Many people choose to garden so they can have control over what type of food they eat without fear of chemicals or preservatives. Often, commercially grown produce is cultivated in greenhouses with the use of pesticides and chemicals to enhance their growth.

A quick study on these types of artificial applications can be unnerving for anyone. The side effects of chemical pesticides on the human body can truly take its toll. So many people are jumping on the "organic bandwagon" as a way to minimize the risks to themselves and their loved ones that often comes with commercially prepared foods.

You don't have to be a health nut to embrace organic gardening. Imagine the wonderful way you'll feel knowing that you are serving foods that were grown all naturally without the risks that come from applying chemical fertilizers and pesticides.

It's easier than you think. If you've been gardening for years or are just beginning to grow your own food, organic gardening can provide you with peace of mind and pride in your produce. Don't have any clues how to start? That's why you're reading this book!

This book will explore the advantages of organic gardening as well as the best way to begin your all-natural garden. You'll get ideas about mulching, weed control, and composting. Plus, some ideas on all-natural pest controls and ways to make sure your garden thrives – without chemicals!

Let's begin our journey into "Ultimate Guide To Organic Gardening"!

CHAPTER 2: THE BENEFITS OF GARDENING ORGANICALLY

As recent as 25 years ago, the idea of organic gardening was considered quite a radical concept. How in the world were gardeners expected to control the weeds, the bugs, and the animals that could threaten a thriving garden without the use of man-made chemicals?

When you think about it, organic gardening is a really simply theory. For years, people have been growing things without the use of chemicals. The early settlers of our country didn't have Miracle-Gro or Sevin Dust and they made out just fine.

It only makes sense that we should be able to apply the same techniques and get the same results as they did today. We should grow food using Mother Nature's ingredients rather than concoctions born in a chemist's laboratory for the good of all of us.

But the interest in organic gardening goes beyond just the benefits for us and our families. There has been a rise in the interest of ecology and concern about the environment that has given new life to the renewed interest in this form of gardening. By using natural minerals and materials, by taking advantage of natural predators, and by recycling garden waste, the home gardener can maintain an organic garden quite successfully.

There are many, many advantages to gardening organically. Probably first and foremost is that Food produced using organic agriculture is more nourishing and more healthful.

In early August, 2001, the British organization, *The Soil Association*, reported that a comprehensive review of existing research revealed significant differences between organically and non-organically grown food. These differences relate to food safety, primary nutrients, secondary nutrients and the health outcomes of the people who eat organically.

Vitamin C and dry matter contents are higher, on average, in organically grown crops then they are in non-organic crops. Mineral contents are also higher, on average, in organically grown crops. Food grown organically contains substantially higher concentrations of antioxidants and other health promoting compounds than crops produced with pesticides.

Many people think that organically grown foods taste better. Also, some foods grown without pesticides produce a higher amount of an anti-oxidant that has been found to reduce the risk of some cancers.

Overall, though, most people who enjoy organic gardening report that the enjoyment they derive is paramount to their decision to eschew chemicals in favor of the all-natural route. Many people like to watch the tender new growth come to full maturity and, as a bonus, you get to eat it!

With organic gardening, you get extra fresh vegetables. Corn on the cob and newly picked peas are especially noticeable, but this trait extends to all vegetables you grow yourself, especially under the organic method. A phenomenon noted by most people when harvesting their very first vegetables from their very first garden is that everyone eats much more of a given vegetable than they would of a similar store bought variety.

You will save money not only by growing your own food, but you can even make a little extra cash on the side by selling your own all-natural foods that are so popular in the grocery stores these days. If you have canned all the tomatoes you can and still have bushels left over, you can take the extra to the farmer's market and sell your organic tomatoes to others who don't have the advantage of their own garden.

For any gardener who still hasn't been convinced about the need to garden organically, here are some statistics that may help change your mind. In March of 2001, the American Cancer Society published a report linking the use of the herbicide glyphosate (commonly sold as Round-up) with a 27% increased likelihood of contracting Non-Hodgkins Lymphoma.

John Hopkins University also revealed that home gardeners use almost 10 times more pesticide per acre than the average farmer and that diseases caused by environmental illness, exposure to chemicals etc., is now the number one cause of death in the U.S. With the EPA's recent phasing out of common pesticides such as Dursban and Diazinon, we are now realizing that many of the chemicals that we thought were "safe" were never actually tested to see what their effect on children, women, and the elderly could be. The time has come to reassess our dependence on pesticides.

However, you may be asking why are chemicals so bad if we've been using them for years and years?

Chapter 3: What Are The Risks Of Chemicals?

We have chemicals in our everyday lives everywhere. Shampoo, toothpaste, many foods, even our clothing all contain or are manufactured with the use of chemicals. Besides polluting the environment, the use of chemicals can be much more threatening. But we're concentrating on gardening and the use of these chemicals on our food. One of the prominent ways chemicals are used in food production is through chemical fertilizers.

Chemical fertilizers are quick-acting, short-term plant boosters and are responsible for:

1. Deterioration of soil friability creating hardpans soil
2. Destruction of beneficial soil life, including earthworms
3. Altering vitamin and protein content of certain crops
4. Making certain crops more vulnerable to diseases
5. Preventing plants from absorbing some needed minerals

The soil must be regarded as a living organism. An acid fertilizer, because of its acids, dissolves the cementing material, made up of the dead bodies of soil organisms, which holds the rock particles together in the form of soil crumbs. This compact surface layer of rock particles encourages rain water to run off rather than enter the soil.

For example, a highly soluble fertilizer, such as 5-10-5, goes into solution in the soil water rapidly so that much of it may be leached away into our ground water without benefiting the plants at all. This chemical causes the soil to assume a cement-like hardness. When present in large concentrations, they seep into the subsoil where they interact with the clay to form impervious layers of precipitates called hardpan.

Many artificial chemical fertilizers contain acids, as sulfuric and hydrochloric, which will increase the acidity of the soil. Changes in the soil acidity (pH) are accompanied by the changes in the kinds of organisms which can live in the soil. For this reason, the artificial fertilizer people tell their customers to increase the organic matter content of their soil or use lime to offset the effects of these acids.

There are several ways by which artificial fertilizers reduce aeration of soils. Earthworms, whose numerous borings made the soil more porous, are killed.

The acid fertilizers will also destroy the cementing material which bins rock particles together in crumbs. Chemical fertilizers rob plants of some natural immunity by killing off the micro-organisms in the soil.

Many plant diseases have already been considerably checked when antibiotic producing bacteria or fungi thrived around the roots. When plants are supplied with much nitrogen and only a medium amount of phosphate, plants will most easily contract mosaic infections. Host resistance is obtained if there is a small amount of nitrogen and a large supply of phosphate. Fungus and bacterial diseases have been related to high nitrogen fertilization, and lack of trace elements.

Plants grown with artificial chemical fertilizers tend to have less nutrient value than organically grown plants. For example, several tests have found that by supplying citrus fruits with a large amount of soluble nitrogen will lower the vitamin C content of oranges. It has also been found, that these fertilizers that provide soluble nitrogen will lower the capacity of corn to produce high protein content.

Probably the most regularly observed deficiency in plants treated continually with chemical fertilizers is deficiencies in trace minerals. To explain this principle will mean delving into a little physics and chemistry, but you will then easily see the unbalanced nutrition created in chemically fertilized plants.

The colloidal humus particles are the convoys that transfer most of the minerals from the soil solution to the root hairs. Each humus particle is negatively charged and will, attract the positive elements, such as potassium, sodium, calcium, magnesium, manganese, aluminum, boron, iron, copper and other metals. When sodium nitrate is dumped into the soil year after year, in large doses, a radical change takes place on the humus articles.

The very numerous sodium ions (atomic particles) will eventually crowd out the other ions, making them practically unavailable for plant use. The humus becomes coated with sodium, glutting the root hairs with the excess. Finally, the plant is unable to pick up the minerals that it really needs.

So, with chemical fertilizers, in short, you have short-term results, and long-term damage to the soil, ground water and to our health.

Another reason to avoid the use of chemicals and pesticides is that long term use of such chemicals can deplete the soil and leave it unable to sustain further growth. In many cases beds of perennials suddenly stop blooming for no apparent reason, and the culprit is often found to be the overuse of chemical fertilizers, herbicides and pesticides.

Chemicals that are applied to plants can often seep into the water supply thus contaminating it. While it's true, our drinking water does go through a filtration process, it's been proven that this process doesn't remove ALL of the harmful contaminants.

It has also been proven that certain chemicals can cause diseases, birth defects, and other hazardous health problems. All one needs to do is watch the movie "Erin Brokovich" to see what chemical contamination of water can do to a body.

Consumers worry about filthy slaughterhouses, e-coli, salmonella and fecal contamination. The CDC estimates that 76 million American suffer food poisoning every year. There are no documented cases of organic meat, poultry or dairy products setting off a food poisoning outbreak in the United States.

Consumers are also concerned about toxic sewage used as fertilizer on conventional farms. Organic farming prohibits the use of sewage sludge.

Consumers also worry about untested and unlabeled genetically engineered food ingredients in common supermarket items. Genetically engineered ingredients are now found in 60 percent to 75 percent of all U.S. foods. Although polls indicate 90 percent of Americans want labels on gene-altered foods, government and industry refuse to label. Organic production forbids genetic engineering.

Eating organic eliminates, or minimizes, the risk from poisoning from heavy metals found in sewage sludge, the unknowns of genetically modified food, the ingestion of hormone residues, and the exposure to mutant bacteria strains. It also reduces the exposure to insecticide and fungicide residues.

Residues from potentially carcinogenic pesticides are left behind on some of our favorite fruits and vegetables - in 1998, the FDA found pesticide residues in over 35 percent of the food tested. Many U.S. products have tested as being more toxic than those from other countries. What's worse is that current standards for pesticides in food do not yet include specific protection for fetuses, infants, or young children despite major changes to federal pesticide laws in

ORGANIC GARDENING

1996 requiring such reforms.

It is certainly in the best interests of the human population to avoid chemicals in our food, but it's also better for our planet as well. Chemicals can affect the soil making it less fertile. They destroy important parts of the natural eco-system. All plants and animals serve some sort of purpose – even if that purpose isn't especially obvious. By taking these components out of the natural life cycle, we are endangering our environment in ways we can't necessarily see outright, but that danger is there.

So it becomes obvious that growing your food naturally is the best way to go. Let's take a moment and look at what exactly organic gardening is.

CHAPTER 4: THE THEORY BEHIND ORGANIC GARDENING

Many gardeners wonder what exactly organic gardening means. The simple answer is that organic gardeners don't use synthetic fertilizers or pesticides on their plants. But gardening organically is much more than what you don't do.

When you garden organically, you think of your plants as part of a whole system within nature that starts in the soil and includes the water supply, people, wildlife and even insects. An organic gardener strives to work in harmony with natural systems and to minimize and continually replenish any resources the garden consumes.

Organic gardening operates on the concept of recycling. You use animal waste, kitchen scraps, and vegetable waste to mulch and compost. You will use common household items like vinegar and soap to prevent pests and weeds.

Organic growers rely on developing a healthy, fertile soil and growing a mixture of crops. Genetically modified (GM) crops and ingredients are not allowed under organic standards.

ORGANIC GARDENING

Organic gardening is the merging together of plants and soil allowing the Earth to naturally bear what it was made to do. The plants and the soil are one working together to provide food and nourishment not only to humans but to animals and organisms as well.

It's not a new age science. It's actually quite simple and can be satisfying to the soul! So let's get more in-depth on getting started.

Chapter 5: How To Plan Your Garden

Your first task is choosing where to plant your garden. The site should receive at least six hours of direct sunlight daily, and the soil should drain well, with no standing puddles. The area should receive adequate air circulation, yet be protected from strong winds. Your house or a thicket of trees can act as a shield from the wind.

After choosing your site, decide how large you want to make your garden. Beware of beginning too ambitiously; tending a plot that's too large can quickly become a chore. A plot 10 feet long by 10 feet wide is large enough for some tomato plants, lettuce, a bush variety of cucumber plant, radishes, an endlessly productive zucchini plant, herbs and some flowers.

Once you've chosen your site, draw out a garden plan; this plan will ensure maximum productivity by giving each plant room to grow. Measure the dimensions of the plot and draw a scale model on graph paper, using, for example, a one-inch square to represent one foot.

As you draw your plan, keep in mind each plant's space requirements at maturity-the little tomato plants you put out in the spring will take up three feet of space by the end of summer. Consider laying out your garden design in blocks instead of the more familiar rows. Because you don't have to allow as much space for paths, this will enable you to plant more.

Blocks containing a variety of plants encourage mini-gardens of vegetables, herbs and flowers, and are more diverse than single rows that alternate just two plants. Single crops crowded together are more susceptible to disease, so the diversity of blocks can mean healthier plants. Make each block just wide enough so you can comfortably reach the middle from each side.

The layout of your garden depends in part on what it is you want to plant. Some crops, such as lettuce, radishes and spinach, mature quickly and will be short-term residents, unless you plant and harvest them several times during the summer. Other plants, such as tomatoes, eggplant and peppers, will grow over the course of the entire season. Perennial herbs and flowers will remain in the same spot year after year, requiring an increasing amount of space each year.

Be sure to save your garden plan to use as a reference for rotating crops next year. Besides depleting the soil of nutrients, leaving plants in the same spot each year encourages disease and soil-borne insect predators. No annual plant should go in the same spot two years in a row. If you wait three years before putting a plant in the same spot, that works even better.

It is a good idea to consider planting "green manure" plants to fix the soil. You can add this to your plan from year to year. Clover, Alfalfa, and other such plants fix nutrients from the soil, which can be used by other plants, as well as adding bulk and organic matter to the soil, when they are dug, or tilled directly into the soil.

Another key to growing organically is to choose plants suited to the site. Plants adapted to your climate and conditions are better able to grow without a lot of attention or input; on the other hand, when you try to grow a plant that is not right for your site, you will probably have to boost its natural defenses to keep it healthy and productive.

Once you plan out your garden for this year, you should really make a plan for next year as well. Because crop rotation is so important to keep healthy soil, as long as you're making a plan, draw up where you will plant what in the next season. This will help you remember what was planted where and save troubles next year.

So now you know where you'll put your garden and what you're going to put in it. Let's get started on the planting!

Chapter 6: Soil Preparation

Proper soil preparation is the key to successful organic gardening. The goal is to feed the soil, which in turn will feed your plants. Begin by testing your soil to find out precisely what you've got to work with. Contact your local Cooperative Extension Service. Most counties and some universities have one; look online under "Cooperative," "Extension" or your county name to find out what is required for a soil test. Home test kits are available at garden-supply stores, but their results are not as accurate or complete.

A soil test will measure pH, the soil's acidity or alkalinity. The recommended pH for a vegetable garden is 6.8. The test results should include guidelines for adjusting the pH, for example, how much lime to add to acid soils or how much sulfur to add to alkaline soils. Both are available at gardening centers.

The test also should analyze the amounts of nitrogen, phosphorous, potassium, calcium and other elements in the soil that are critical for healthy plants. The testing agency may suggest nutriments to balance these elements; when you mail off your sample, be sure to enclose a note stating that you intend to garden organically so the tester does not suggest chemicals.

Some of the nitrogen sources the tester may suggest can be problematic, especially for vegetarians: Bone meal is a slaughterhouse byproduct, fish emulsion is a fish-processing byproduct, cottonseed meal is subject to heavy pesticide use and urea, or crystallized animal urine, is so processed it can no longer be considered even remotely natural. If nitrogen is a problem for your soil, and you are opposed to using animal byproducts, your best bet may be to plant a nitrogen-fixing cover crop this first year and start your vegetables the next.

When gardeners speak of a soil, they are referring to earth that looks, feels and smells pleasant. That means fertile soil, with good structure depending on the extent to which the inorganic soil particles; sand, silt, clay, and humus are bound together. No matter what kind of miserable soil you begin with, it can be transformed into the stuff great gardens are made of.

You also should test the soil's percentage of organic matter, or decomposed plant material. There are different levels of consideration according to your area that will determine if a soil is organic. The best organic matter to fertilize your garden with is compost. As a new gardener, you may not have compost of your own yet, but more on that a little later in the book.

Composting involves recycling of natural matter like vegetable peels, coffee grounds, and egg shells. All of these will provide nutrients to the soil that a successful organic gardener knows are of paramount importance!

When you till up your plot, work in some loose topsoil along with natural organic matter into the existing soil. Horse or cow manure will work the best here. Find a local farmer and ask if you can buy some dung from him. If you don't have any of these available to you, most local garden centers will have some natural additives that you can till into the soil. You can also use leaves or grass clippings.

By tilling this organic matter into the soil, the organic material will form moisture-holding humus in the soil and the loose structure will permit good drainage. Plus, it can provide needed nutrients to your plants and help them thrive as they grow.

You can make your own organic fertilizer as well. You'll get a couple of great "recipes" in later sections.

Be careful that you don't dig up your plot too soon in the season. Cool spring soil holds moisture, and disturbing wet soil will damage its structure. We found one tip online that can help you determine whether or not your soil is ready for tilling.

Jim Crockett, former Public Broadcasting System gardener extraordinaire, suggests that before digging you take "the chocolate cake test": If the soil has the consistency of moist chocolate cake, it's safe to dig. If it's more like fudge, wait until the soil has dried out to cake consistency.

Soil is structured in layers, and it's best not to disturb those layers. Dig down just far enough to remove clods of grass, weeds and root masses, shaking and pounding out as much dirt as possible back into your garden. Save the grass for composting.

After the dirt is prepared, let the garden rest for a couple of days before planting.

It's almost time to plant!

Chapter 7: Planting Your Organic Garden

You can choose to buy plants that are already growing that can be found at most garden centers, but if you do this, you can't be sure what pesticides have come in contact with these plants. Your goal, as an organic gardener, is to avoid these chemicals, so we recommend starting your garden from seed.

If you want to simply plant the seeds directly in the ground, that's fine, just remember that growing from seed takes a little more time than growing from plants, so be patient!

Don't get too over-anxious here! Many beginners will take a seed packet and dump its contents into the ground hoping a few plants will spring up. What they don't realize is that with care, they will probably ALL come up – or at least most of them.

The problem here is that these plants will strive for air and light developing tall, weak stems and they will not thrive as they choke each other out.

There are some plants that can be seeded thickly. These include peas, parsnips, radishes and bush beans. It's fine to block these together as they will grow fine in clumps.

Seeds have within them everything they need to grow, except moisture and warmth. But, if you pile 4-inches of soil over them they will be overwhelmed. The soil is heavy and cold and often damp enough to rot off the emerging leaf bud before it can break the surface. Be kind to your seeds. Cover them with soil to a depth no more than 2-times their size. Very fine seeds shouldn't be covered at all.

There are also some vegetables that are conducive to early planting. These include radishes and leaf lettuce. They tend to come up quickly and can be harvested before any of your other plants have even begun to bud.

With these types of plants, plant a single row or small bed and keep replanting every two or three weeks in small amounts. You'll take up the same amount of space, save harvest time, and have a continuous crop throughout the growing season.

When planting your seeds, you'll need to dig a small trench and sprinkle them evenly throughout the row. The rows should be at least an inch apart, but increasing that distance make for easier weeding and gives you walking space between the rows.

As we said, sprinkle them evenly and try to avoid crowding. In other words, don't just dump the seed packet in the trench. You must leave room for the plants to grow and be able to get adequate light and air circulation.

Once they're in the ground, mark what you have planted where. Use a Popsicle stick with the plant name written on the front and stick it in the ground at the beginning of the row. This way once the plants start to bud, you'll know where to look for them.

Water well after you've planted your seeds and then wait. You'll soon begin to notice small plants popping through the soil and reaching for the sun. Before long, with proper cultivation, you'll have beautiful plants!

Sometimes, it's more satisfying to start your seeds indoors in the winter time so that when the spring arrives, you'll have your own organically grown starter plants ready to put into your garden plot. Let's look at how to start your seeds indoors.

Chapter 8: Start Your Seeds Inside

Starting your seeds indoors will lessen the amount of time you have to wait to see results in your garden, and many people prefer to grow their plants indoors first to ready them for the growing season. It can be motivational and satisfying.

If space is available near a sunny window, start seeds four to eight weeks before the plant-out date in your area (average date of last killing frost). Starting too early usually results in spindly plants due to crowding and lack of sufficient light.

Almost any container with drainage holes in the bottom will work for planting. Paper milk cartons cut in half, Styrofoam cups, tin cans, plastic trays and pots are common containers used. For convenience, however, you may wish to start plants in the plastic trays and pots available at garden supply centers.

Use a rich, well-drained soil. Potting soils made for African violets and other house plants usually are suitable and do not have weed seeds. They are, however, more expensive than soil mixes you can make at home. If you use soil from the yard, it should be top soil that is well drained and not high in clay.

The best soils are often found around established shrubs and trees. Add sphagnum peat and sharp sand to the soil in a ratio of about one-half volume of each, and mixed thoroughly.

To kill weed seeds and some damaging soil fungi present in your commercial soil, place the soil mix in shallow trays or baking pans in an oven for 45 minutes at 250 degrees. For best results, the soil should be moist.

After the soil has cooled, fill containers firmly but do not pack. Allow about 3/4 inch from the soil surface to the rim of the container. Place seeds on the soil surface. Use a piece of window screen or old flour sifter to sift soil over the seeds to the depth indicated on the seed packet.

If you use compartmentalized trays or individual peat pots, place two or three seeds in each pot. Do not cover too deeply, as this may reduce or prevent seed germination. Just like planting directly in the ground, a general rule is to cover no more than four times the diameter of the seed.

Apply a fine spray of water to avoid washing the seed, causing them to float to the soil surface. Household window sprayers are suitable.

Cover the containers with plastic sheets or panes of glass and place in a cool room (60 to 65 degrees) away from direct sunlight until germination. By doing this, you will almost eliminate the necessity of watering the bed again before the seeds germinate. Be sure to keep an eye on it though. DON'T let it completely dry out!

Germination can take anywhere from a few days to a couple of months, depending on what you are growing, so patience will have to be on of your virtues.

When seeds germinate, move them gradually (over two or three days) into brighter light. When the seedlings have developed the first true leaves (the leaves above the cotyledons or "seed leaves"), thin to one plant per container if using partitioned trays or peat pots. Use tweezers to pinch off unwanted seedlings rather than pulling them, to avoid disturbing the remaining seedling.

If seeds were planted in larger containers, transplant into individual peat pots or other small containers. An alternative is to thin the seedlings so they are spread about 1 1/2 to 2 inches apart and leave them in the larger containers. This method, however, makes inefficient use of seed and space.

Water your seedlings carefully. Small containers used for starting plants dry out quickly. On the other hand, soil kept soaking wet inhibits seedling growth and may kill the plants.

About one week prior to planting-out time, gradually expose seedlings to longer periods outdoors unless temperatures are below 50 degrees. At the same time, reduce watering to a minimum as long as plants do not wilt. This will help the plants adjust to full exposure without undergoing undue shock at planting time.

When it comes time for planting in the ground, carefully remove the plant from its container keeping the roots intact. Dig a small hole in the garden plot and place the plant into the hole. Cover up the roots completely nearly up to the bottom leaves of the plant. Pack down the soil around the plant and water!

CHAPTER 9: ORGANIC CONTAINER GARDENING

If you do not have enough yard for a regular organic garden; you can still grow plants and vegetables organically; by doing container gardening.

What To Use As A Container

When it comes to what to use for a container, when growing an organic container garden; you are only limited by your imagination. Keeping true to the concept of organic; some organic gardeners only use natural containers. For example, they would select containers constructed out of wood or clay. However, you do not have to be obliged to this concept.

If the container can hold dirt and can accommodate getting wet, it can be used. For example, an old pail, wheelbarrow, and even a worn-out shoe could be utilized for your organic container gardening needs. The only other stipulation to the type of container used, besides holding dirt, and being able to get wet; is the container must also have proper drainage holes. Most organic plants will not do well if they get too much water. That's why it's essential, the container be able to drain water properly. If the container isn't suitable for this; you can always drill holes into the bottom of it

Whatever container you choose to use, for your organic plants, it's important to put about an inch of broken clay pot pieces or gravel into your container. If you're so inclined, you may also add leaf mold or pieces of ripped out newspaper, on top of the gravel. The reason for using leaf mold is to ensure the soil retains some moisture. The gravel further aids in proper drainage of water from the container.

What Type Of Soil Should Be Used When Growing An Organic Container Garden?

When growing an organic container garden, you should begin with 100% organic soil. Organic soil is soil which has no man-made chemicals in it. You can purchase organic planting soil from an organic garden supply store.

The biggest disadvantage to having an organic container garden is the lack of subsoil. The organic soil you choose must be able to retain water, and not let your organic plants get too wet. A good way to ensure your organic plants don't get excessively wet is to use peat moss as an additive to your organic soil. The best type of soil mixture, to provide to your organic container garden plants, should be comprised of all the following ingredients: organic soil, compost (see the section on making your own organic compost), composed manure, and peat moss.

What Type Of Organic Plants Can You Use In Your Organic Container Garden?

You can plant the same organic plants in a container garden that you could plant in a regular organic garden. For example, you can plant any of the following; Beans, tomatoes, peppers, lettuce, herbs, or eggplant. This, by no means, is an exhaustive list of what can be planted; in an organic container garden. The only word of caution; the container has to be able to hold whatever plant or vegetable you put into it. Remember, a cucumber will still occupy the same amount of space, in a container, on your porch, as it would a hole in the ground.

Just as you should start your regular organic garden with organic seeds, you should do the same when growing an organic container garden. When it comes to pest control and organic container gardening; the same methods can be used as mentioned in the organic pest control section. Best of all, pest control in an organic container garden requires much less effort.

Even if you don't have a large yard for an organic garden, you can still grow chemical and pesticide free vegetables and plants. All you need it is an area that receives adequate light, a sheltered area, and a container large enough to hold the organic plant of your choice. Thanks to organic container gardening; you can enjoy fresh vegetables year round.

Chapter 10: Organic Hydroponic Gardening

The best part about hydroponic organic gardening is you don't need soil to grow an organic garden. However, this concept can be confusing. As discussed previously, part of what makes organic gardening; organic gardening, is using organic soil. If you don't have organic soil, how could it be an organic garden? This section will show you why hydroponic organic gardening can be advantageous over regular organic gardens.

The key to organic hydroponic gardening is the water. The organic plants get their nutrients from the water, not soil. Organic plants, even hydroponic ones, can't grow until they have a solid substance to put their roots into. You can grow organic plants hydroponically by putting them in vermiculite and perilite. A word of caution is in order: When handling vermiculite, the utmost care must be taken.

This is because vermiculite is a form of asbestos. You can also use organic materials such as straw, cotton, plant fiber, or any number of other organic materials.

Preparing The Water For Your Hydroponic Organic Garden

Since the water is the sole source of your organic plants nutrition and not soil; your organic plants must have nutrient rich water to feed their roots. Since the goal is to grow an organic garden, all nutrients dissolved, in the water, must be organic. One such nutrient commonly used in organic hydroponic gardens is what is referred to as "compost tea." Compost tea is created when compost is put into water. The water is infused with the organic compost material. Once the organic compost has been fully saturated by the water, the water is then strained. It is necessary to strain the water because any solid compost material remaining must be removed. What's left, after the water has been strained, is an organic, nutrient rich, water; which your organic plants will love to drink.

You can also make what is commonly referred to as manure tea. However, it can be dangerous to make your own manure tea. There is a risk of getting bacterial contamination on your organic hydroponic garden vegetables. You could actually contaminate your vegetables with lethal strains of E. Coli. The manure used for manure tea should be thoroughly broken down through decomposition.

You can also create manure tea with sterilized manure. The process to make manure tea is the same as you would use to make compost tea. Other common organic materials, which can be combined with the water, include seaweed and fish emulsion.

The other advantage to hydroponically growing your organic garden is you won't waste water. The nutrient rich water can be continuously used on your plants. In other words, unlike a traditional organic garden, the water used is not wasted. The nutrient rich water, used to feed your hydroponic organic garden, isn't used one time and then thrown away. You should keep recycling the nutrient rich water to feed your plants; over and over again.

As you can see, an organic hydroponic garden can be a more practical, viable, solution compared to growing a regular, organic

ORGANIC GARDENING

garden. It is true; you won't get the same "earthy" experience a regular organic garden would provide. After all, there is no "earth" to dig in. However, you will still get the same delicious, chemical free, home grown, organic vegetables.

Chapter 11: Weed Control

Weeds can be an organic gardener's curse. Actually, for all gardeners, weeds are the bane of their existence in some cases. This author absolutely detests weeding her garden, but it must be done to promote healthy growth of plants and insure a good crop.

Even if you're not an organic gardener, weed control is a problem. There really is no easy answer to this problem. It just takes time and effort to control the unwanted overgrowth in your garden. This is where mulching and composting come into play.

First of all, twice a week, run the edge of a sharp hoe just under the surface of the soil to behead tiny weeds before they grow large enough to compete with your seedlings.

Once the seedlings are larger, the soil is warm and drenching rains have ended, put down a layer of mulch to hold in moisture and smother weeds. Mulch is material that can be laid down around the plants to control weeds.

Choose ingredients that allow the soil to breathe, let water in and keep light out. These can include dried--not fresh--grass clippings, chopped straw, lawn-mower-chopped leaves mixed with dried grass clippings or well-rotted sawdust (avoid fresh sawdust, as it leaches nitrogen from the soil), and pine needles are all good choices. Apply the mulch several inches thick.

Be warned that if you use grass clippings or weeds, you run the risk of bringing insects or diseases into the garden if these are not composted. Either of these types of mulching can become incubators for insects, so it's best to compost them before using as mulch.

A thick layer of mulch keeps light from reaching weeds. Without adequate light, the plants don't produce enough chlorophyll to enable further growth. Most of these plants sicken and die before you even notice them. The few plants that do manage to stick their leaves into the light will be shallowly rooted and very easy to pull.

Organic mulches—straw, grass clippings, leaves, shredded bark—nourish the soil as they decompose. They are fairly effective weed barriers.

You can also apply a layer of compost to control weeds. Be warned that if you use kitchen waste to make your compost, you could have some "volunteer" plants that crop up. One of my neighbors was pleasantly surprised to find cherry tomatoes growing where she had composted. She included discarded tomato seeds in her compost pile and these seeds germinated on their own making a really nice little surprise crop for her!

If you live in a wet climate, you may wish to avoid mulching and keep cultivating, because mulch can lead to waterlogged soil and fungal diseases. In a climate subject to dry spells, mulch can dramatically reduce plant stress by helping the soil retain moisture. If you irrigate, feel under the mulch to be sure the water is getting through.

Mulch is great, but there are two ways to misuse it. One is to mulch heat-loving plants too early in the season, before the soil warms up. Mulch smothers weeds, but it's also a good insulator.

Cantaloupes, tomatoes, potatoes, watermelons, peppers and egg plants will produce better if mulched.

Another mistake is to put down too little mulch. It looks good for a few weeks, but then weeds poke through, and they must be hand pulled, for there's just enough mulch covering the ground to make hoeing impossible. Insufficient mulch gives your plants much less drought protection.

How much is enough? Well, maybe this will give you an idea: Sawdust; 2 to 3-inches / Shredded leaves; 8 to 10-inches / Straw; 5 to 7-inches / Newspaper; 4 to 7-inches / and Grass Clippings; 5-inches when you first spread them.

Another way to control weeds is through various ground covers. This is often called "soil solarization". Soil solarization involves placing thick plastic sheeting on top of the weeds and allowing the natural sun to "bake" the weeds until they die. This can take some time, so you must be patient!

Many people prefer to use newspaper for their ground cover. Because the paper will naturally decompose, it is environmentally friendly as well.

Simply place 4-5 layers of newspaper in between your plants and cover with a light layer of dirt so they don't blow away! By covering up the weeds, you will be better able to control them!

Also consider Kraft paper – like grocery bags – or cardboard. By using Kraft paper and cardboard, even less light can reach the weeds and makes the cover even more impenetrable.

You can suppress the growth of weed seeds early in the season by spreading corn gluten meal over the area where they're growing. Corn gluten meal, a by-product of corn processing that's often used to feed livestock, inhibits the germination of seeds— bear in mind, once the weeds have gone beyond the sprout stage, corn gluten will not affect them.

Be wary, however. Corn gluten doesn't discriminate between seeds you want to sprout and those you don't want, so avoid using corn gluten meal where and when you've sown seeds. It works best with established plants.

Unfortunately, you will have to employ some old-fashioned methods to weed control in your garden. It can't be avoided.

Hoeing is a huge part of a successful garden. Annual weeds die when you sever the stems from the roots just below the soil surface. With a sharp hoe, you cut the weeds easily. You may want to eschew the traditional square headed hoe for this job and try an oscillating one.

To hoe your garden without cultivating a backache, hold the hoe as you would a broom—that is, with your thumbs pointing up. Skim the sharp sides of the hoe blade through the top inch of the soil.

You will also have to do some hand-pulling of those weeds. It doesn't have to be back-breaking work, though. It just takes persistence.

Here's the trick to comfortable, quick weed-pulling:

Put your hands in front of you, thumbs up and palms facing your body, one hand in front of the other. Now roll your hands, like kids do when singing "This old man goes rolling home."

Pinch your forefinger and thumb together as you reach the outermost edge of the imaginary circle your hands are tracing and move your arms to the side as you roll your hands. With practice, you will be surprised by how quickly you clean up a row in the garden with this movement.

Finally, organic weed control can be done easily by placing common household vinegar in a spray bottle and apply to those weeds. Vinegar is the organic equivalent of the commercial Round-Up, so be careful when applying around thriving plants.

Beside those incessant weeds, you'll also need to worry about pest control.

Chapter 12: Pest Control

For the natural gardener, pest control might seem like a daunting task. After all, you're committed to not using harmful chemicals in your garden, yet these chemicals can get rid of pests quickly and easily.

There are still many ways you can take control of your garden without resorting to chemical treatments. Natural pest control is actually quite easy.

We certainly understand that many gardeners become anxious when they see pests on their plants and want to react decisively when they see their plants damaged. But we must remind you of the central principle of organic gardening: growing plants in harmony with Nature. And insects, even those that eat your plants, are a crucial part of that system.

When you see insects in your garden, take some time to really watch what they're doing. Are they actually destroying the plant or just nibbling it a bit? Many plants can outgrow minor damage.

Also, in many cases, insects attack stressed out plants. Do you have enough healthy plants to spare the sickly ones? Can you restore sickly plants to robust health so they can resist insect attack?

The best defenses against insect attack are preventative measures. Grow plants suited to the site and they'll be less stressed out. Don't let them be too wet, too dry or too shaded. Design a diverse garden, so that pests of a particular plant won't decimate an entire section of the garden. Healthy soil will naturally produce plants that are resistant to insects and disease, but pests are a part of gardening.

There are different ways you can control pests naturally.

SPRAYS AND POWDERS

There are a number of natural botanical sprays and powders available in garden centers. These are derived from plants and not made in a lab. We'll look at a few of the more common ones available to you.

Insecticidal soap is sodium or potassium salts combined with fatty acids. If you use soap, it must come in direct contact with the insect and it must be wet. It is no longer effective once it has dried.

The fatty acids in the soap penetrate the insect's outer covering and cause the cells to collapse. This is one of the safest organic pesticides to use because there is no residue, it is non-toxic to animals, and you can use it on your vegetables all the way up to harvest. Be cautious, however, soap can burn or stress plants, so don't use it in full sun or high temperatures.

Bacteria spray is also commonly known as Bt *(Bacillus thuringiensis).* There are more than 80 types of Bt used as pesticides. It is a stomach poison that releases toxins in the stomachs of insects that causes them to stop eating and starve to death.

It is generally available in powdered form that is sprinkled or dusted on a plant. It must be eaten by the targeted insect. Bt strains are very host specific and will not harm people, pets, birds or bees, but it can be very slow acting taking days for the insect to completely stop eating and die. It can also kill some of the beneficial insects in your garden.

Neem is a spray that is derived from the seed kernels of the neem tree fruit. It is sprayed onto the plant's leaves which will upset the insect's hormonal system and prevents it from developing to its mature stage. Neem is most effective on immature insects and species that undergo complete metamorphosis.

Use caution with Neem as it can be damaging to pets, so keep them away from freshly sprayed leaves until the liquid dries. Neem is non-toxic to humans.

Horticultural Oil is highly refined petroleum oil that is mixed with water and sprayed onto foliage. It coats and suffocates insects or disrupts their feeding.

There is a low toxicity to humans, pets, and birds and does not leave behind any toxic residue. Be careful you don't burn the leaves of your plants when you use this oil.

Rotenone and Pyrethrum are most readily available ones and are often used in combination. They are derived from the roots of tropical legumes. It generally comes in powder form that is dusted onto the plant. These will inhibit the cellular process thus depriving insects of oxygen in their tissue cells. This is a broad spectrum pesticide and can be used with many types of pests.

If you are using a spray, dilute it in water and use only as needed. Of course, follow application directions on the label. The best time to apply sprays and powders is in the evening or in early morning. And always read the labels of anything you buy commercially. Just because a pesticide is organic doesn't mean it isn't toxic.

You don't HAVE to use anything on your plants if you depend on other animals to help you control pests.

ANIMALS AND BUGS

Birds, ladybugs and praying mantises are the gardener's best friends when it comes to insect control.

Birds can be encouraged into the garden by feeding, hanging a birdhouse providing a bird bath or by planting plants that provide berries for them to eat.

Ladybugs are now for sale by the pint, quart or gallon. The average-sized garden can get by on a quart or less, as there will be about 25 to 30 thousand bugs per quart. The cost is generally less than five dollars a quart. The average adult ladybug consumes between 40 and 50 aphids a day.

Praying mantis cases are also available and each one hatches up to 400 young. The cost is rather nominal for a case. A few gardeners have reported that this insect disappears rather rapidly from the garden, so you might want to experiment with just a few to begin with. They will eat any insect they can catch.

Frogs and lizards can also control pests by eating them. You can make your garden hospitable for your natural allies by keeping a water source – just a dish full - nearby for them and by not wiping out the entire pest population with a pesticide, sending the beneficial elsewhere in search of food. Also, grow plants with small blossoms like sweet alyssum and dill, which attract predatory insects who feed on flowers' nectar between attacks on pests.

Organic pest control is a comprehensive approach instead of a chemical approach. Create a healthy biodiversity so that the insects and microbes will control themselves. Using natural products and building healthy soil is the best long-term treatment for pests.

What are the pests you should be looking for?

Chapter 13: Common Garden Pests

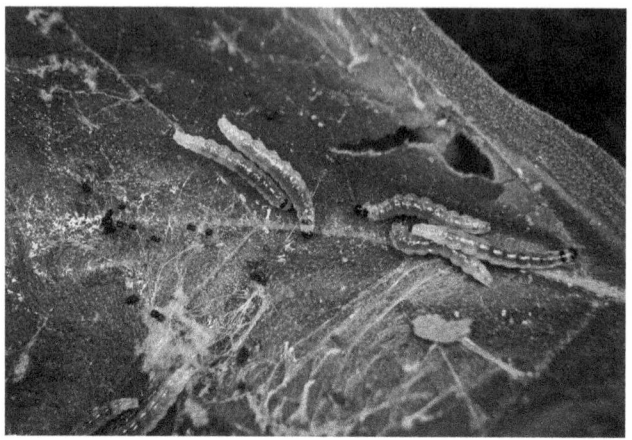

There are literally hundreds of common garden pests that can attack your plants and threaten the viability of your gardening efforts. We couldn't possibly address all of them. There are, however, some that occur in more frequency than others.

Aphids are probably the most common problem in gardens. Aphids are soft, pear-shaped, and very tiny (1/16 to 3/8 inch long). Two short tubes project backward from the tip of their abdomen.

Aphids have long antennae. Some types of aphids have wings, which are transparent, longer than their body, and held like a roof over their back. Aphids may be green, pink, yellowish, black, or powdery gray. Nymphs resemble adults but are smaller and wingless.

They feed in colonies, so where there's one, there's definitely more. Aphid feeding can cause leaves to curl and become deformed. Once this has happened, the aphids are protected from any treatment you give to the plant, so it's important to attack the problem as soon as possible.

Many species prefer the underside of leaves, so look there first. Ants are usually present where aphids are, so if there are ants in the garden, there are probably aphids as well. Aphids are the ant's food source, so they will protect that food warding off predators that might threaten them.

To naturally control aphids, first be sure to drench plants with strong sprays of water from a garden hose. Keep your plants as healthy as possible, and spray dormant oil to control over wintering eggs. You can also spray plants with insecticidal soap, summer oil, and homemade garlic sprays. At the end of the book, we'll have some recipes like this for you to make yourself.

If you will be growing cabbage, broccoli, or cauliflower, you could have cabbage loopers. These pests are light green in color with white stripes running down their back. The larvae can reach approximately 1½ inches long and have three pairs of slender legs near the head and three pairs of larger legs at the rear end. The middle section is legless and is looped when the insect is moving.

The larva is the damaging stage of the cabbage looper. The young larvae feed between the veins on the undersides of leaves. Large larvae make ragged holes in the foliage and move to the center of the plant where feeding generally occurs at the base of the cabbage head. Large loopers can also burrow through three to six layers of tightly wrapped head leaves.

The best way to control cabbage loopers is to handpick the larvae a few times a week. Attract predatory and parasitic insects to the garden with pollen and nectar plants.

If you find small holes in the leaves of your plants, you may have earwigs. Earwigs are generally dark brown, slender and elongated. They have a pair of "pincers" at the rear of their body and they run more than fly. They have a curved up abdomen and release foul odor when disturbed.

Earwigs will eat holes in the leaves of plants causing them to wilt and die.

In general, earwigs can be beneficial to your garden, but they can get out of control, so you should use the general spray you'll get later in the book. There are a number of ways to control earwigs, but trapping them is probably the best way to eliminate them from your garden.

One way we like is to take a shallow dish and place beer in it. Any beer will do. The earwigs will be attracted to the beer, climb in, drink, and die. You can sift out the dead ones and reuse the beer for trapping again. They are also attracted to corn oil, fish oil, or water and vinegar. You can place these in dishes just like the beer.

If the leaves of your plants are finely speckled with yellow spots or a silvery, metallic sheen, you could have thrips. Thrips are very small – about 1/16" - and difficult to see. There are many varieties of thrips and they are of all different colors.

Thrips are best controlled with sprays as we've described. You can also spray the plants with soapy water. Lady bugs will eat thrips as well, so attract those lady bugs to your garden!

Tomato hornworms are the largest caterpillars found in this area and can measure up to 4 inches in length. The prominent "horn" on the rear of both gives them their name.

Hornworms are often difficult to see because of their protective coloring which is green. Not much for the heat of direct sunlight, they tend to feed on the interior of the plant during the day and are more easily spotted when they move to the outside of the plant at dawn and dusk

Hornworm damage usually begins to occur in midsummer and continues throughout the remainder of the growing season. The size of these garden pests allows them to quickly defoliate tomatoes, potatoes, eggplants, and peppers. Occasionally, they may also feed on green fruit. Gardeners are likely to spot the large areas of damage at the top of a plant before they see the culprit.

The best way to control hornworms is to handpick them off your plants. They are especially susceptible to the Bt bacterial spray we described above, so we strongly suggest using this to control your hornworms.

Slugs are among the most troublesome pests in the garden. They feed on a variety of living plants and decaying plant matter. On plants they chew irregular holes with smooth edges in leaves and can clip succulent plant parts. They can also chew fruit and young plant bark.

Because they prefer succulent foliage, they are primarily pests of seedlings, herbaceous plants, and ripening fruit such as strawberries, artichokes, and tomatoes that are close to the ground. However, they will also feed on fruit of some trees, citrus is especially susceptible to damage.

Slugs are nocturnal and come out at night. They slither under rocks and leaves in the day. Holes chomped into leaves and fruits are telltale signs of slug feeding. A more certain sign of slug activity is the silvery trail of dried mucous that these pests leave in their wake. If that's not sufficiently convincing, go out into the garden at night with a flashlight and surprise them.

Slug control is actually quite easy. They are rather large, so they can be caught by hand and disposed of. This is another garden pest that be caught by setting out a dish of beer.

While possibly cruel, the most effective way to kill a slug is to sprinkle it with salt. You can trap the slugs by placing a plastic bag in the garden containing two decaying lettuce leaves, 2 cups of bran cereal, and pouring beer over the whole mess. Put the bag out before sundown. In the morning, check to see if the slugs are in there and dispose of them.

Prevent slug infestation by removing dead and decaying leaves. This will remove their primary food source. Coffee grounds and egg shells will also keep slugs away. Just place them around the plants you want to protect at ground level.

Chapter 14: How To Make Your Own Compost

Composting can be as simple or as complex as you want to make it. The best part about creating compost is that it can consist of any organic material and we all have access to plenty of that every single day because it is produced by the lawn, garden, and kitchen.

Compost is what happens when leaves, grass clippings, vegetable and fruit scraps, woodchips, straw, and small twigs are combined, then allowed to break down into a soil-like texture. Compost introduces and feeds diverse life in the soil, including bacteria, insects, worms, and more which support vigorous plant growth.

Compost is multi-faceted but not intended as a fertilizer. It offers only a relatively low proportion of nutrients, yet what it does is close to magical. In its finished form as mulch, it reduces evaporation, reduces or prevents weed growth, and insulates the soil from extreme temperature changes. Mulch also keeps the upper inches of the soil cooler in daytime, warmer at night.

Yet compost has humble beginnings. Common, easily accessible materials destined to decay together in a pile will give your soil the gift of minerals and other components it needs. The materials are indeed numerous.

Regardless of the particular ingredients, making compost is akin to making bread or beer; soil-digesting bacteria like yeasts need warmth, moisture, air and something to feed on to keep them alive and growing. Almost all of the practical problems associated with making compost stem from too much or too little of those basic factors.

Compost is created from layers of grass clippings, leaves, weeds, kitchen scraps and, if available, farm animal manure. If you have meat eaters in your home, don't use their meat scraps, which will attract rodents. Also, do not use litter from your dog or cat; it doesn't break down properly and contains too many pathogens.

Over the years, composting has gotten a reputation for being a time-consuming job, but this is not necessarily the case. You don't need to build a big box or turn the pile every so often. A barrel, a hole in the ground or a pile on top of the ground is satisfactory.

The important requirement is to be sure the waste material is covered with soil, so it doesn't attract rats, other rodents or flies. You can build your layers directly on the ground, without any frame at all; if you use a container, be sure it is well ventilated.

The trick to successful compost is balancing ingredients high in nitrogen-fresh grass clippings, other fresh, green plant matter, most kitchen scraps--with those high in carbon--leaves, straw, dried grass, washed eggshells, wheat germ or other milled grains that have become too rancid or old to use, and any dried, brown plant matter. Too much nitrogenous matter yields an anaerobic, smelly pile. Too much carbonaceous matter results in a pile that never heats up. The ideal ratio is one part nitrogen to three parts carbon.

Start with a layer of brush-small twigs, no large branches-a couple of inches deep; this will help your pile to breathe. Then, keeping in mind the 1 to 3 ratio of nitrogen to carbon, add a layer of mixed plant material. You may enrich the pile with horse or cow manure. These materials don't break down; they simply add nutrients to the final product.

Then lightly water the pile so it's evenly moist. Too much water will interfere with aeration; too little water and the pile won't ferment. If your pile sits in the open, you should pull a tarp over it before a storm, and then remove the tarp after the rain stops so the pile can breathe. An 8-inch layer of straw mulch spread over the top of the pile serves the same purpose.

Alternate layers until the pile is 5 feet high by 5 feet wide by whatever length you choose. A properly made pile that is loosely packed and well aerated will reach an internal temperature of 160 degrees within a few days. It should smell like wet hay. If the pile fails to heat up, pull it apart and redo it by adding layers of fresh green matter. If the pile becomes anaerobic (is too wet to aerate), pull it apart, let it dry out, use it as mulch and start a new pile.

After three weeks, the pile will have shrunk in size; this is normal. Dig into the pile with a spading fork and completely turn it over until the contents are redistributed; the idea is to put unfermented particles in contact with those that are further along. Let the pile rest, so the temperature will rise again. Turn it a second time five weeks later, let it rest a few weeks and, with luck, you'll have a rich, crumbly pile of "black gold."

Also, air is vital to any composting process. Without air (anaerobic) composting is possible but unpleasant with the putrescent of rotting material assaulting your nose. It is usually because there is too much nitrogen and too little air in the mixture. If you have an abundance of trees on your property, autumn leaves can be plentiful and messy, but they are there for your use and can be easily gathered and stored in leaf bags.

Timing is crucial. Your pile is fully composted when it fails to heat up after being turned. Then it is ready to use. And use it with a good feeling, for it is your garden's natural fuel. Remember your objective, the foundation of every successful garden, is to achieve healthy soil.

Compost supplies the soil with a rich, friable source of humus and helps retain moisture in the garden, in addition to supplying valuable nutrients. By placing grass clippings, fallen leaves and unused plant parts in a compost pile, you are preparing them, through decomposition, to be put back to work for you.

Composting actually recycles garden waste and returns the nutrients that have been taken from the soil. By using organic composting agents, it is possible to speed-up the process of decomposition.

Now that you've gotten that garden in, how do you take care of it?

CHAPTER 15: TENDING YOUR GARDEN

You've spent quite a bit time and effort to make sure your garden is laid out in the most promising way and considering how best to grow that garden organically. Now you need to take care of your plot.

Plants need light and water to grow. The light is already taken care of by Mother Nature; you have to take care of the water!

Watering the garden every evening after dinner can be good therapy for the gardener, but it's not good for the plants. When the soil is often sprinkled on top but never deeply soaked, plant roots tend to remain in the damp, upper few inches of soil where they are vulnerable to searing mid-summer heat and drought. Vegetable plants need an average of 2-inches of water a week. Be sure to water thoroughly so the soil is soaked to a depth of 4 to 6-inches. This will encourage roots to grow deep.

Germinating seeds and seedlings need to be kept uniformly moist without being washed away, so water them with a gentle spray every day or two. Developing plants need to be watered deeply, but less often, to encourage deep root growth. Water to a depth of at least 6 inches and then let the surface inch or two completely dry out before watering again.

As a general guideline, garden plants that have been watered properly, and therefore have developed deep roots, need a thorough watering every 5 to 7 days in hot weather.

Hand watering delivers water directly to the plants, thus eliminating waste, but it takes time. Spot check to make sure you are delivering enough water, and be careful to give all areas of the garden adequate coverage.

Sprinklers have the disadvantage of wasting water by watering paths and other open spots in the garden. They also lose water to evaporation and wind drift. Because they wet the foliage, sprinklers also can promote the development of leaf diseases.

However, sprinklers are easier and eliminate the need to stand outside holding a hose for 20 minutes – especially if you have a large garden.

If you use oscillating sprinklers, elevate them above the tallest plants so the water streams are not blocked. To make sure all of your plants are watered, place sprinklers so their patterns overlap. Runoff indicates you need to water at a slower rate.

You can also consider taking a simple garden hose and making your own irrigation system by poking holes in the top of it at uniform angles. Simply place this hose between the rows of plants and move when the watering is done in that particular section.

You should generally water your garden in the early evening when it is cooler. This will reduce the chance of evaporation from the hot sun and heat. Early morning watering is fine, but less effective.

Be wary of over-watering your garden. This can cause your plants to be less successful and produce disappointing yields. Generally, the first few weeks after planting and transplanting and during the development of fruit or storage organs are times when plants may be adversely affected by shortages of water, so water plentifully during these times.

ORGANIC GARDENING

Obviously, Mother Nature will provide you with some of her water as well. Monitor your rain levels and check to be sure that your garden has enough moisture if it has rained to see if you need to add to it.

Healthy plants that produce a wealth of healthy food can get a well needed boost from some type of fertilizer. Composting can provide this, but there are other ways to fertilize.

One of the best sources of organic fertilizer is animal manure. Cow, chicken, rabbit, horse and mink are among the most readily available in many parts of the world. It is best to use them after they have had a chance to rot for a few years. They provide some plant nutrients, favorable bacteria, humus, better aeration and they help retain more moisture when they are mixed with your garden soil.

Manures are available from dairy farms, riding stables, and poultry farms. Usually you will have to pick them up from these sources, using your own truck. Sometimes firms that deliver soils or mulches will also stock and deliver one or two types of fresh or well-rotted animal manures. A check of the want-ad section of the newspaper will often reveal additional sources of supply.

If you use fresh manures, they are best applied in the fall, as they are apt to burn or retard plants if they are applied during the spring, growing season. Well-rotted manures can be used in the spring. You should apply the fertilizer around the base of the plant.

You can use either fresh or rotted manure to make a liquid-tea to feed plants. The tea is usually made of one part of manure and ten parts of water. Let it set for several days before you use it then spray directly on the plant.

The process-dried manures are often available at garden shops and can be used for top-dressing or they may be mixed into the planting soil. Fish meal, blood meal, bone meal, animal manures, cottonseed meal and processed sewage sludge are organic sources for nitrogen fertilizer. Phosphate rock and bone meal are the two organic fertilizers used to supply phosphorus. Wood ashes and rock potash are the two main sources of organic potassium.

Your local garden department will generally stock any of the above organic fertilizers. You can also make your own fertilizer from the recipe section of this book.

When it comes to fertilizers, seed meals and various kinds of lime are the most important ingredients. These alone will grow a great garden. Seed meals are byproducts of making vegetable oil. They are made from soybeans, flaxseed, sunflowers, cotton seeds, canola and other plants. Different regions of the country have different kinds more readily available. Seed meals are stable and will store for years if kept dry and protected from pests in a metal container with a tight lid.

Lime is ground, natural rock containing large amounts of calcium, and there are three types. Agricultural lime is relatively pure calcium carbonate. Gypsum is calcium sulfate and is included because sulfur is a vital plant nutrient. Dolomite, or dolomitic lime, contains both calcium and magnesium carbonates, usually in more or less equal amounts. If you have to choose one kind, it probably should be dolomite, but you'll get a better result using all three types. These substances are not expensive if bought in large sacks from agricultural suppliers.

Organic fertilizers are much more conducive to the environment and the health value of our foods than the traditional chemical fertilizers. Why?

Organic fertilizers, manures and composts release their nutrient content only as they decompose - as they are slowly broken down by the complex ecology of living creatures in the soil. Complete decomposition of most organic fertilizers takes around two months in warm soil. During that time, they steadily release nutrients.

With non-organic fertilizers, overdosing can be a real problem. They are so strong that it's easy for inexperienced gardeners to cross the line between just enough and too much.

Yet, despite their strength, inexpensive blends are incomplete. They supply only nitrogen, phosphorus and potassium. Unless the manufacturer intentionally adds other essential minerals, the chemical mix won't supply them. Chemical fertilizers rarely contain calcium or magnesium, which plants need in large amounts along with tiny traces of several other minerals.

Inexpensive chemical fertilizers dissolve quickly in soil. This usually results in a rapid burst of plant growth, followed five or six weeks later by a big sag requiring yet another application. Should it rain hard, the chemicals dissolved in the soil water will be transported as deeply into the earth as the water penetrates (this is called "leaching"), so deep that the plant's roots can't reach them. With one heavy rain or one too-heavy watering, your fertile topsoil becomes infertile. The chemicals also can pollute groundwater. The risk of leaching is especially great in soils that contain little or no clay.

Chemical fertilizers can be made to be "slow-release," but these sorts cost several times as much as those that dissolve rapidly in water. The seed meals in an organic fertilizer mix are natural slow-release fertilizers, and they usually are less expensive than slow-release chemical products.

You should fertilize your plants once every three to four weeks. You will want to pay attention to how your plants are doing and fertilize accordingly. Some plants need more fertilization attention than others.

Beans, peas, and carrots are among the low demand vegetables for fertilizing. They need fewer requirements for additional nutrients than the medium demand plants.

Most garden plants are medium demand plants. These would include tomatoes, corn, squash, zucchini, cabbage and peppers. Be careful not to over-fertilize these plants. A good rule of thumb is 4-6 quarts of fertilizer per 100 square feet with a ¼ inch layer of compost.

Some high demand vegetables are artichokes, cauliflower, turnips, and spinach. These will require the same 4-6 quarts of fertilizer per 100 square feet, but you need to increase the compost layer to ½".

High-demand vegetables are sensitive, delicate species and usually will not thrive unless grown in light, loose and always-moist soil that provides the highest level of nutrition.

Of course, you need to stay on top of the weeding to insure your plants have enough room to grow and that those weeds don't steal away their food!

It's best to tending the garden at the same time every day. Morning would be best since it is cooler during the summer and you won't have to bear the oppressive heat. Don't let the weeds take control. This is why we recommend doing so every day so that you won't have a huge job if you neglect it for a week or so.

Taking care of a garden might require you to get on your hands and knees to pull weeds from the middle of your bean plants or cabbage rows, so do this. It'll save stress on your back and, of course, bring you closer to the natural environment that is your organic garden!

Then just sit back and wait for the benefits of your garden – fresh produce! Of course, the successful gardener knows that once cold weather arrives, their job isn't quite done.

Chapter 16: Preparing Your Garden for Winter

Never leave your garden bare over the winter, because it will lose organic matter through oxidation. Plant oats at the end of the harvest and let them die over the winter, or cover the garden with leaves and straw. As soon as the ground freezes, mulch perennial herbs and flowers heavily to keep frost from heaving them out of the ground. Pull the mulch off in early spring to let the ground become warm and dry.

Once you have harvested all the fruit you can and your plants have gone dormant, till all the plants under with a tiller. This will provide the soil with organic material to nurture it for next year.

Apply a thick layer of your compost and till again. It's a good idea to till one more time prior to planting when the ground isn't frozen, of course. By doing this, you'll gain control of any possible weed problems, plus you'll be working in more compost to make the soil prime for planting next spring.

Chapter 17: Bring Your Organic Plants Indoors For Year Round Growth

Most organic plants can be grown almost effortlessly indoors. The best part about growing your organic plants inside is the control you'll have over their growing environment. For example, they will be better protected against harmful garden pests and insects. You can grow your organic plants year around by growing them inside.

How to transition your outside organic plants for inside growing

This is not as complicated as you may believe. One of the most critical components to this process is choosing hardy plants to bring inside. By the time the spring and summer growing seasons are finished, you'll know which plants are good candidates to be brought inside.

You must prepare these plants for the indoors, before the first frost hits. The first step is to extract these plants out of the soil. You're going to need to ensure when you extract the plants, the entire root is intact. This means you're going to have to dig deeply into the soil, to make sure you get the whole root. Once you have your organically grown plants extracted, roots and all, transplant them into new potting soil right away. Ideally, the root balls should have 2 inches of potting soil surrounding them, inside the pot.

You'll want to carefully inspect your organically grown plants, to be sure there are no harmful insects clinging onto them. If you find any, pluck them off and spray your plant with Once insect inspection is completed and any pests are taken care of; give your organically grown plant a good watering.

There is a hardening off process that you must prevent, prior to transporting your organic plants inside. You can do this by placing them in an area which does not get a lot of direct sunlight. You should tend to your organic plants for a week. You are training them to get used to the lack of direct sunlight. During this week of training, you must keep them watered, trimmed, and properly pruned.

Once the one week training period is over, you may bring your organically grown plants inside. Typically, the rule of thumb is to give your new indoor plants five hours of light a day. If you don't have anywhere, in your living space, that gets this type of lighting, you'll have to give them artificial light. You can accomplish this with a fluorescent light, which is positioned approximately 6 inches suspended above your organically grown plants. You should leave this light on, for the plants, 14 hours a day.

You must also make sure your organically grown plant is protected from the cold, while it is inside. Don't let the temperature your plants are exposed to, drop below 60°. If your organic plants experience too frigid of a temperature, they will not fare very well. Also be sure you keep your organic plants out of drafty areas.

Your organic plants should also have a lot of moisture. You need to keep them damp by using gravel trays and keep their pots in water. Keeping your organic plants growing inside, year round, is easy to do. The most essential part to keeping them indoors; year round, is to try and replicate optimal growing conditions, they would experience outside, while they are inside. If you bring your organically grown herbs inside, it's important to know they prefer humid environments.

Now let's look at those recipes promised to you!

Chapter 18: Natural Recipes For Your Organic Garden

You don't have to purchase commercially produced organic products for your garden. Many can be made by you with a minimum of effort. Of course, you'll have to buy the ingredients, but we can assure you that in the long run, it'll be much cheaper than buying those other products.

Organic Fertilizer

To concoct the fertilizer mix, measure out all materials by volume: that is, by the scoop, bucketful, jarful, etc. Proportions that vary by 10 percent either way will be close enough, but do not attempt to make this formula by weight. An old 5-gallon plastic bucket will allow you to stir up about 14 quarts.

Mix uniformly, in parts by volume:

- 4 parts seed meal
- 1/4 part ordinary agricultural lime, best finely ground
- 1/4 part gypsum (or double the agricultural lime)

- 1/2 part dolomitic lime
- 1 part bone meal, rock phosphate or manure
- 1/2 to 1 part kelp meal (or 1 part basalt dust)

Farm feed and grain dealers are the best sources for large bags of seed meals, which are typically used to feed livestock. The other ingredients usually can be found at garden shops, although they probably will be sold in smaller quantities at higher prices per pound. You may find the best prices by mail order or on the Internet.

Garlic Pest Control Spray

Many cultures around the world have used garlic as a natural antibiotic and anti-fungal remedy. When garlic is combined with mineral oil and soap, it becomes a very effective pest control product.

However, when it is sprayed, it is not a selective insecticide. It can be used to control cabbageworm, leafhoppers, squash bugs, whitefly, but will also affect beneficial insects so be careful where and when you apply this product.

- 3 ounces finely chopped garlic
- 2 tsp mineral oil
- 1 pint water
- ¼ ounce liquid dish soap

Allow the garlic to soak in the mineral oil for 24 hours. Add water and liquid dish soap. Stir well and strain into a glass jar for storage. This is your concentrate.

To use: Combine 1-2 tablespoons of concentrate in 1 pint of water to make the spray. Do be careful not to make the solution too strong. While garlic is safe for humans, when combined with oil & soap, the mixture can cause leaf injury on sensitive plants. Always test the lower leaves of plants first to make sure they aren't affected.

Dormant Oil

The purpose of an oily spray is to suffocate over wintering pests, such as aphids and mites. Most commercial products are made of kerosene or other petroleum oil. A much less toxic and more sustainable approach is to use a renewable resource such as vegetable oil.

- 1 cup vegetable oil
- 2 tbsp liquid soap
- 1 gallon water

Combine the soap and oil and stir to blend thoroughly. Add the water a bit at a time, stirring as you go (water and oil don't really emulsify; the soap helps the process). Pour the mixture into a clean garden spray container. Spray a coat of the mixture over the entire plant. Shake the container frequently as you are spraying.

This recipe makes 1 gallon.

Homemade Insecticidal Soap

Soap has been used for centuries as an all-purpose pesticide. It disrupts insects' cell membranes, and kills pests by dehydration. The key is not to use too much soap, or you'll also kill the vegetation near the pests. If you follow the proportions of soap to water in the Soap Spray recipe, below, the vegetation should be fine.

1 to 2 tablespoons liquid soap (not detergent)

- 1 quart water
- Combine ingredients in a bucket, mix, then transfer to a spray bottle as needed

All Purpose Pesticide Soap Spray

Strong smelling roots and spices such as garlic, onions, horseradish, ginger, rhubarb leaves, cayenne and other hot peppers, are all known to repel insects.

- A handful of roots and spices
- Boiling water to cover the roots and spices
- Soap Spray (recipe, above)

Add the roots and spices to the bottom of a mason jar. Cover with the boiling water, screw on the top, and let set overnight. Strain, and add to the Soap Spray. Note that this will rot, so use it all up or freeze leftovers for another time.

Place into a spray bottle and apply to the plants to control pests.

Bug Juice

Although it seems a bit macabre, consider using bug juice to fight pests. Some scientists believe that pheromones from blended insects send a warning to their living relatives. While this has been tested, it isn't a fool-proof method, but it's something worth trying!

- 1/2 cup of pesky insects
- Water

Place the insects in an old blender with enough water to make a thick solution. Blend on high and strain out the pulp using cheesecloth or a fine sieve. Dilute at a rate of 1/4 cup bug juice to 1 cup of water, pour into a spray bottle, and apply to plants.

Chapter 19: Conclusion

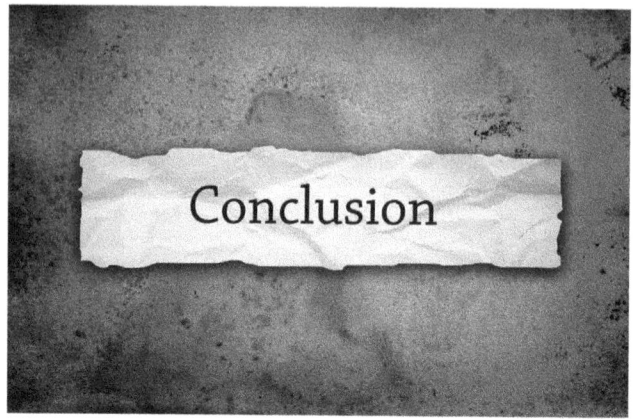

Gardening in any form is therapeutic and relaxing not to mention a way to enjoy success as you bite into the first ripe tomato of the season. When you choose to go organic, you are making a choice to protect the environment as well as your family when you grow your own food.

While most of this book has been directed toward vegetable gardens, the same concepts can be applied to flower gardens. Going organic is so important to the Earth as we need to preserve our natural resources and insure we have a healthy place to live.

Try getting your children involved in gardening as well. Nurturing plants from seed to harvest inevitably leads to increased feelings of confidence, self-esteem and pride. One only has to see the beaming face of a child who has harvested their first carrot to appreciate the value of this experience. The child becomes empowered and motivated by the realization that hard work and patience produce concrete, satisfying results.

Consider providing your child with his or her own garden plot. Don't make it too big and plant a few different types of vegetables. We would suggest a tomato plant, a carrot plant, a couple of beans, and perhaps a watermelon. You will be teaching your child valuable, valuable lessons as they tend to their own garden and experience the "fruits" of their own labors!

For some children gardening may offer merely the excitement of watching seeds grow and harvesting the bounty. For others it offers the opportunity to develop skills they would build on as adults, leading possibly to a rewarding hobby or career.

Above all, gardening is fun and is a skill that, once acquired, can be a lifelong companion. It is not a skill that must be mastered to be enjoyed, and it is extremely adaptable to diverse needs and abilities.

Organic gardening, however, is so much more satisfying. The soil that feeds us is something we should think about every day. The way we treat that soil is something else we should consider – every single day.

The life cycle is a beautiful thing and all creatures were put here for a reason – even the garden pests! Natural people want that natural cycle to keep rotating.

The health benefits of organic gardening are many, but the emotional benefits are so much more. By going organic, you will know that you are doing everything you can not only for Mother Earth, but also for your family. We should all strive for the natural pleasures that we have been given.

And yes, growing things in the dirt is one of them! Happy gardening!

The following websites were referenced in researching this book:

www.wikipedia.org
www.theorganicgardener.com
www.organicgardeningtips.com
www.goingorganic.com

Meet the Author

Gardener and Landscaper James Gipson has spent his last couple decades bringing beauty into the world, whether it's in his own back yard, the neighborhood playground, or over many acres surrounding a corporate office building.

In his twenties, James started a small lawn and landscaping company to make money while he was writing the great American novel. He did write his book, but what started as a necessary evil evolved into a viable—and joyful—business. Turns out James has a way with plants and soil, and soon his little company was in high demand. It wasn't long before he was hiring help and showing 5-year plans to investors. During his years in landscaping, he brought his green thumb to just about every type of garden project, but his very favorites were local parks. For James, true fulfillment was found in expressing his art while benefiting the community.

Three years ago, James gave his back a break and retired, but he still keeps up with the garden and greenhouse on his own property. Because neighborhood is important to him, he sits on his homeowner's board and is known as the "Flower Man" to the kiddos on his street. He also consults with the local park district and village boards as they beautify the parks, streets, and municipal buildings.

James lives in Tulsa, Oklahoma, with his wife of 43 years. They are blessed with a hoard of grandchildren, and fill their gardens with Easter Eggs every April. He believes families are a lot like flowerbeds—if you cultivate goodness, you usually get goodness. And he is very thankful to be living the good life.

MORE BOOKS BY JAMES GIPSON

The Urban Gardening Guide: How to Create a Thriving Garden in an Apartment, On a Patio, Balcony, Rooftop or Other Small Spaces.

Vegetable Garden Basics: Grow Your Own Vegetables and Save Money

www.ingramcontent.com/pod-product-compliance
Ingram Content Group UK Ltd.
Pitfield, Milton Keynes, MK11 3LW, UK
UKHW022120230426
12048UKWH00010BA/628